The Heart Speaks to The Mind

Wisdom Stories from the World's Great Masters

Amarjit Singh Modi & Elizabeth Temple

iUniverse, Inc.
New York   Bloomington

Also by the Authors

Discover Your Divine Destiny and Live with Joy

Christ: Mother Mary's Gift of Light

The Heart Speaks to The Mind

Wisdom Stories from the World's Great Masters

With guidance from

Buddha
Christ
Hinduism
Socrates
Tolstoy
and more

Retold and interpreted by renowned psychic

Amarjit Singh Modi & Elizabeth Temple

iUniverse books may be ordered through booksellers or by contacting:
iUniverse

1663 Liberty Drive
Bloomington, IN 47403
www.iuniverse.com
1-800-Authors (1-800-288-4677)

ISBN: 978-1-4502-1434-6 (sc)
ISBN: 978-1-4502-1435-3 (ebook)

Printed in the United States of America

iUniverse rev. date: 04/07/2010

*May all who share this planet
experience greater happiness
through greater understanding
of all that exists.*

Contents

Introduction

At some time in your life you have had the experience of reading a very special story, or listening as it was told to you – a story that had an everlasting impression on your mind and continues to affect the way you live today. Everywhere in the world we travel, people offer us this kind of wisdom in the form of stories that are important to them, and share with us their profound influence on their daily choices.

We listened to their individual experiences, and to the valuable messages they convey to every person who wants to learn from the wisdom of the past, and we selected some of the most beautiful to share with you. Some of these stories have been written in books, and some have been passed from person to person for hundreds of years in the land of their origin, or performed as plays or dances. We also uncovered some new stories which have deep and profound meaning in our lives, and inspired us to write this book.

Discovering these precious gems gives us great joy, and we hope that people from every continent can benefit from the collective wisdom of humankind. In our humble way we give some stories' meanings and their applications, but please make your own interpretations in a way that makes sense to you to apply to your life. We offer these stories to you as an everlasting gift that you can cherish and share with your friends. If you understand their meaning, accept them, and act on them, your life will be transformed!

Inspire like an angel,
Live fully as a human,
Share your love with all.

Acknowledgements

We thank the wise people of the past who allowed us to share this wisdom with you, and who are a constant source of guidance for all who are willing to listen and learn.

We thank the writers who have kept the stories featured in this book alive through the centuries, including but not limited to: authors, translators, and editors of the *Bible*, the *Dhammapada*, and *Shiva Purana*, translators of the works of Leo Tolstoy and Plato, and storytellers of Indian and Persian folktales.

Our eternal gratitude to you!

Attachment Invites Suffering

There was a priest who lived near the river Ganges. Every morning he went for a walk and then to the river to take a bath. His friend the yogi met him at the river at the same time each morning, and there they spoke on various practical and philosophical topics before going off to their jobs.

One morning as he walked, the priest counted the repairs that needed to be done to the temple, and wondered where he could ever find the money to pay for them. After his walk he went to bathe in the Ganges, and there a magnificent thing happened. He stepped into the water and saw a large diamond shining at his feet, just under the surface! He could not help but pick it up. It was obviously a precious diamond, and its natural beauty filled him with joy. He held it up in the light, and turned it this way and that to admire every angle of its perfection. Then the diamond slipped from his hand and fell back into the river. In half a moment it was swept away.

The priest began to cry.

Just then his companion the yogi came to the river, saw him and said, "I never see you cry here in the morning, what has happened?"

He said, "Something extraordinary has happened. I found a great clear diamond in the bank of the river! I held it in my hand but a moment before it fell into the water, and now it is lost forever!"

The yogi said, "But that's fantastic. Look, you are no worse off than you were, in fact you were blessed to hold and appreciate it, as you said, 'today something special happened,' so I do not understand why you cry."

The priest said, "I cry because I lost my diamond! It came to me, I held it in my hand, and now I've lost it! How beautiful it was!"

Then the yogi said, "You are mistaken, my friend. What came from the river went back to the river. How can you be surprised? You did not lose your diamond, for it never belonged to you!"

———————

The priest in the story suffered because he began to possess the gift life gave him. This is an excellent story to remember when you suffer loss of any kind. When we grieve over a loss we can make ourselves suffer more than necessary by thinking that we lost what was ours. The yogi tells the priest that he never owned the diamond; that something which did not belong to him in the first place merely returned to its origin.

If someone you love dies, understand that all along they came from the universe as a gift. The person who died cannot help but leave; they did not die in order to harm you, therefore they did not wrong you by leaving. It is only natural that we go back to where we came from.

Remember this story to relieve your pain whenever you lose something very precious. If you lose your house in an earthquake, you can remember that the house was not really yours! The house came from the earth and from human labor. Your house only went back to the earth, and another one can be built with more labor. If your boyfriend or girlfriend leaves you, you can relieve your suffering by asking yourself, "Was that boyfriend *mine*? Did I create him?" The answer will be 'no'—that friend came to you as a gift from life, and they have only walked back out into life.

We suffer when we attempt to possess the gifts life gives us rather than celebrate them. The priest in the story celebrated the beauty of the diamond every moment that he held it, and he did not need to regret having this experience. We should celebrate the gifts in our lives every moment that we hold them, knowing that they do not belong to us, but to life itself. We should appreciate the people we love every day, and enjoy them to one hundred percent of our ability. Then we can know we did not miss one opportunity. With the yogi's perspective, under even the greatest loss, you can maintain your peace of mind.

Acceptance of Negative Gifts Invites Pain

Buddha used to speak with his disciples each evening. They came to ask him questions and to clarify their doubts. Buddha addressed their concerns when no one else could, and so many people liked Buddha and treated him well. But one evening a man came into the meeting and immediately began to curse and abuse Buddha. He called him vulgar names, and insulted his life's work.

Buddha kept quiet and listened for a long time, until the man had no more to say. Then he said calmly, "Brother, can you come and sit, and talk together with us?"

The man was amazed to see Buddha so peaceful. He thought, "Somehow all my abusive language did not make him angry."

Then instead of hating Buddha, he asked him, "How is it possible that you are not angry with me?"

Buddha said, "Do you bring presents to your relatives when you visit them?"

"Of course," he said, "I always bring a gift."

"And what would you do if they rejected your gift?"

"I would take it back home with me," he said. "I would keep the gift myself if they don't want it."

Then Buddha said, "All these curses and abuses you brought to me as a gift, but I do not accept them, so please take them back home."

Wow! This story can help every person regardless of their beliefs, because a Buddhist can be angry, a Muslim can be angry, a priest can be angry, anybody can be angry. Becoming angry is a common response to the common situation of being presented with anger. Buddha's response is quite uncommon, but he used it 2,500 years ago, and many psychologists use it today to help their patients.

Everyone can benefit from this knowledge: pain, anger, and hatred that someone offers you remains with them if you do not accept it. The pain came from the person who gave it to you, not from you. If you accept the gift of pain it will burn you, but you are not obligated to accept it. This is a timeless problem, and a timeless solution that really works.

Let's address three applications of Buddha's solution:

First, Buddha's solution relieves the suffering of your past. If you did not receive enough care from your parents, if you were not loved when you were young, you can learn from Buddha that you do have a choice in the matter. Sometimes, due to ignorance, parents fail to provide a positive environment for children to grow up in their home. Either they don't offer the love that children need, or they curse and scold them, or they physically or sexually abuse them. The child carries their suffering deep in their subconscious mind—as children there is nothing else that we can do. But when you grow up and remember this painful time, you have two choices: you can curse and abuse the people who abused you, and in doing so continue your suffering, or, you can return those negative gifts and set yourself free to live a new life with your own free mind.

There is no reason to accept the abuse you received! Abuse was not on the list of gifts you wished for as a child. You did not ask for it, therefore it is not yours to claim. The painful gift was always the property of the other person, so return it and claim your happiness. If you don't, the abuser is getting what they wanted—they succeed in making you suffer. It doesn't matter if it was your parent, sibling, neighbor, it doesn't matter who that person was. What Buddha tells us is that the feeling and experience they offered you belongs in their life, not in yours. It is your choice to adopt the experience and make it your own, or to acknowledge the true owner and turn it away. This is something we cannot know as children, which is why the pain of childhood lasts into adulthood. But as adults, all those who received abuse as children must return the negative gift to the person who gave it. Then you will be free from past suffering. Say, "No thank you, you can keep your pain, it is not for me!"

Next, apply Buddha's solution to every lack of blessing, not only mistreatment in childhood. Maybe you were born in the wrong country, under an oppressive government. Maybe you didn't have good teachers in school, or maybe you were born without money. The people who put this grief in your life are not thinking about your suffering; they may not even be aware of it. Now you must decide how to respond. Instead of arguing against suffering that was inflicted upon you without your consent, like Buddha you can calmly decline to suffer! If your friends or family turn against you, if society doesn't accept your creativity, if your religious or political leaders fill your head with intolerance and hatred for yourself or for people of other backgrounds, you are free to refuse those negative ideas. You are free to retain your inner happiness, to keep your mind unsoiled, open to positive ideas, and to enjoy your life in the way *you* see fit.

Gifts of pain, neglect, and limitation are not what you need, and you will only suffer for as long as you decide to accept those ideas as your own. In fact, every curse in the world is only a lack of love, and we can reverse this lack of love with our choice. So, no matter how many abusive ideas you have been offered, you can reject those teachings and still appreciate yourself, knowing that the pain of the people around you does not need to belong to you.

And finally, in your personal life, if someone rejects your love and you accept this rejection, you may hurt yourself by thinking that you are unworthy of love. You could make yourself physically sick, you could get lonely and depressed, you could neglect your work, and could gain weight. You could cause your own spirit and body to wither, and subsequently make yourself unfit to love! Then you can learn from Buddha that you have a choice: either accept this negative energy and suffer, or choose to keep the gift of your love and find someone else who will accept it. This way you can avoid all the negative consequences described above, and keep your heart ready to love again.

Please don't wait for any particular person to come along in order to express your love. Love your dog, love your mother, love your grandmother while she is still alive! Or give your love to nature by loving plants and trees. Then you will keep your life alive, you will keep your heart healthy and intact, and you won't get discouraged, because you will know that you are capable and valuable. If someone tells you that you are not good enough, just say, "Okay, that is what you think." But don't accept it! Who wants a gift like that? Just because someone said it does not mean that it is true. The person who said it is just a person. Maybe they, too, are suffering from this lack of love. Now you know how to counteract it.

Listen to this scripture from the *Dhammapada*:
"He abused me, he beat me, he defeated me, he robbed me—in those who harbor such thoughts hatred will never cease."(verse 3)

Then we hear the good news:

"He abused me, he beat me, he defeated me, he robbed me—in those who *do not* harbor such thoughts hatred *will cease*." (verse 4, emphasis added)

The moral of the story is that when someone is angry at you and you don't get angry, only he suffers, not you. When someone causes you pain, and you chose not to cause them pain in return, their pain burns them, instead of burning you. If you don't want to suffer, do not accept abuse as your own. You are not obligated to accept any gift, so return the harmful ones to the sender. You get much more than money back—you get your freedom!

"Conquer the angry one by not getting angry; conquer the wicked by goodness; conquer the stingy by generosity, and the liar by speaking the truth."

Dhammapada, verse 223

The Dancer Transforms The Demon

In India, God is worshiped in three aspects of creative power: Brahma for birth, Vishnu for life, and Shiva for death. Lord Brahma is the giver of life, Lord Vishnu is the provider of all we need in life, and Lord Shiva is the destroyer, breaking life down so that it can begin again. This is a story about a demon who aspired to possess the power of Lord Shiva. The demon thought of nothing but Lord Shiva's power to destroy. He prayed to Shiva many times a day, and at night until the moment he fell asleep. He professed Lord Shiva's greatness everywhere, and honored him with devotion beyond any Shiva had ever received.

Lord Shiva heard the demon calling for one year, and then he came to pay him a visit. He appeared in the form of a man to the one who praised him and said,

"I am Shiva, the one you worship faithfully. Tell me, why do you pray so fervently, and for so long?"

The demon clasped his hands together, bowed down and said, "All I pray for, Lord, my only desire, is a power so great as yours. Give me the power that when I touch someone on the top of their head, anyone I choose, instantly they will turn to dust."

Lord Shiva said, "What a strange thing to ask."

The demon stood up and said, "But this is what I want. This is the only blessing in the world that will satisfy me. I will keep praying to you forever."

And so Lord Shiva touched his forehead and blessed him, giving him the power he asked.

Immediately the demon lunged at Shiva and tried to catch him! Lord Shiva jumped and took off running and the demon ran after him into the jungle. You see, as soon as the demon felt Shiva's power within him, he realized that it could destroy Shiva, too! He seized his one opportunity to turn Lord Shiva into dust, rid the world of the God of destruction, and become the only person with his terrible gift. This is what the demon thought as he chased Shiva through the jungle.

Lord Vishnu saw Lord Shiva running for his life and came to assist him. (These three creative Gods work together, and they always know the status of their companions.) Lord Vishnu appeared among the trees in the form of a dark-haired woman in a long flowing dress. When the demon ran by he stopped to admire her. Lord Vishnu then stepped forward and greeted him, giving Shiva time to escape.

The demon forgot about catching Shiva. He was too busy enjoying his good fortune—here the most beautiful woman he had ever seen was acknowledging him, on the same day he received the power of God!

Quickly he wiped the sweat from his forehead and asked, "Would the lady be so kind as to dance with me?"

The woman who was Vishnu said, "I will dance with you if you follow me. Whatever movements I make, you must make those same movements, and then we can dance together."

The demon agreed and they began to dance. Now, try to imagine the exquisite way God can dance in the form of woman. She began with a gentle swaying motion of her waist. The demon watched her and followed along, and he felt his body begin to cool and relax. After a minute he felt quite tall and graceful, like a tree swaying in the breeze. Then Vishnu began to make some soft steps with her feet. The demon watched the beautiful curving steps and found that he could easily make his feet do the same, and what a pleasure it was! All of his attention was fixed on Vishnu; faint music seemed to come from her body. Slowly Vishnu began to move her arms in the most elegant patterns. The demon was caught up into the intricate paths of her hands and fingers. He placed one hand gently into the other the way she did, and with delight he saw the shape of a certain flower he loved. He reached with Vishnu to the sky, and felt as light and free as the birds perched in the branches high above. He watched her caress her lovely smooth cheek, and when he did the same, he felt that his own must be just as beautiful. He watched her touch her hand to the top of her head like the coronation of a queen, and then he was gone! The demon was no more!

For he had touched his hand to the top of his own head, and instantly he turned to dust. From then on, this man was called Bhasmasura, which means 'the demon of ashes.'

This story teaches us two lessons about destructive power. The first lesson is that actions meant to harm another can just as easily harm oneself. The second lesson is that destructive desires lose their power when we experience joy.

The demon in the story represents any regular person. A "demon" simply means a person who is causing pain. All people temporarily turn into demons when we desire to harm or control another. But be careful! Destructive power destroys everyone involved. The blow you intend for your enemy can just as easily destroy yourself or the people you love.

Consider the leader of a country who destroys their own people by sending them to war and having them killed! It is the same mistake for a parent to mistreat their child and destroy their own family, and for a business manager to mistreat their employees to the detriment of their own corporation. This selfish misuse of power is self-destructive. The demon teaches us to be careful not to misuse our power.

Lord Vishnu represents the pleasures and richness of life. When Vishnu invites the demon to dance, she reminds us that we can only enjoy life's pleasures by joining in and giving ourselves over to them. The demon followed along and became so involved in dancing that he forgot his power entirely, and forgot its conditions.

There is incredible healing power in creative activities such as dance. When you dance, or sing, or in any way give yourself over to pleasure, you cannot possibly wish to cause pain! Joy elevates us far above selfish and fearful concerns. In this expanded state we forget our limited existence and leave behind our desire to control. So the next time you feel like a demon, participate in any creative activity in which you can feel joy! This will connect you to the source of life, and you cannot stay connected to destructive urges at the same time.

The story of the demon and the dancer contains two pieces of wisdom. The first: the power to harm destroys those who wield it equally as well as the intended target. The second: a person in the midst of a joyful experience cannot wish to harm anyone. Or, as William Shakespeare wrote:

"The man that hath no music in himself,
Nor is not mov'd with concord of sweet sounds,
Is fit for treasons, stratagems, and spoils."

Embrace Christ and Be Free

A man named Mark hurried up the road to attend his Sunday morning church services. If he didn't hurry he was certain to be late, and he wanted to arrive before the priest closed the door. Then Mark saw Jesus Christ standing by the side of the road and stopped in amazement to look at him. "Of all the days to meet Jesus," thought Mark, "of course it would be the day that I'm running late for church!"

Jesus said, "Hi, Mark. Where are you going in such a rush?"

Mark said, "I'm going to church, to wash away my sins and my guilt. I pray to you there, and your grace sets me free."

Jesus said, "If you like, I can set you free from sin and guilt right now."

Mark was very relieved and grateful and he said, "Thank you! Of course, I know very well that you do this."

Then Christ placed his hands on Mark's head, said a blessing, and set him free right then and there. Mark thanked Jesus again, and they shook hands and parted. Then Mark was very excited to experience the salvation Jesus granted him, so he ran the rest of the way to church.

When he arrived, the priest met him at the door.

"And why are you late for services?"

The story came running out in one long sentence.

"I was doing my best to get here on time, but on the way I met Jesus and he asked me where I was going, and I said I was going to church to pray to him to forgive my sin and guilt so I can be a free man, and Jesus said, 'I can take that sin and guilt away' and he took it away! So now I'm here, and now I can see what it feels like to be free from sin."

The priest was very impressed. Not once in his long career had any member of his congregation told him of an experience like this. The priest stood in the doorway between Mark and the people inside, and thought about what had happened. In the meantime Mark caught his breath, and made to enter the church. But the priest stood in his way and prevented him from entering.

He said, "Mark, listen, I don't think you need to come to church. You've been set free. Those whose sins and guilt are still with them are inside praying for forgiveness. You have this, so you don't need to come inside. Go share your freedom with others today." Then the priest shook his hand, and closed the door.

––––––––––

Those who are familiar with Christian scriptures know that this story does not appear in the Bible. This is one of my own! I like it very much; it simply says that when you have been freed, go free. Once your chains have been removed, there is no need to remove them again and again. Instead, go enjoy your freedom and put it to use in life.

The man in the story was concerned with ridding himself of the guilt that held him back, and yet when he met Jesus he could not see that his salvation stood right there before him! This was because Mark did not really believe that freedom was possible, and so he continued to church as before. Even after he got the message from Jesus himself, he did not understand that his freedom was real until the priest helped him to see.

This is a good story for religious persons, those for whom the blessing of forgiveness is readily available through their faith. Sometimes, even when a past regret is forgiven, or a restriction is removed, we don't believe that we are truly free of it, so we continue to behave as if we are still held back! We should accept the grace available to us and move on. To embrace Christ is to embrace the light, to know that our forgiveness is real. If we don't accept our release from the burdens of the past we will continue to struggle for no reason, and miss out on the new life we prayed for.

This story says that when an error of the past has been resolved, it is time to close the door, leave it behind, and move on to something better. Isn't it wonderful? We can discontinue working with all problems that have already been solved!

How Did the Universe Come into Being? Buddhist Answer

Buddha's student said, "Great teacher, I must know the ultimate insight, I must know the answer to the question of the very nature of the universe. How did it all come into being?"

Buddha took a deep breath. His student prepared himself to receive what would surely be the greatest wisdom of his life or anyone's.

Buddha said, "In my travels from town to town, I came to a certain village and saw a group of people gathered around a man lying on the ground. Naturally I was curious, and I went into the crowd. The man on the ground had been shot in the chest with a poison arrow.

His brother was there and he demanded, 'Who shot my brother?' Then the people started questioning each other.

'Who shot this man's brother?'

'Did you see the culprit?'

'Was it a man or a woman?'

'Was he Chinese or Indian?'

'Tall or short, or medium height?'

'It could have been God, or the devil.'

'Why would anyone shoot your brother?'

'Does he have any enemies?'

'How could this have happened?'

Then I said, 'Before we answer these questions, let's take him to a physician and remove the poison arrow right away. Otherwise he will die before we find out who shot him. If we save him he may tell us what happened, and if we lose him the answer will not satisfy anyone.' So they picked him up and took him to the doctor."

Buddha stopped speaking. His student looked at him with a blank face. What in the world was his teacher talking about?

Buddha explained.

"Asking how the universe came into being is like asking who shot the arrow. What we must attend to is life." Then the student understood.

This is one of the best stories from Buddha's life, a very small story with a very great meaning. The tale Buddha tells his student is easy to understand: the injured man would lose his life if the people around him did not attend to him quickly. If they succeeded in healing him they might learn the answers to their questions, and even if they never found out who shot it him, it mattered very little in comparison to saving his life. When Buddha's student seeks to discover the origin of the universe, Buddha tells his story to say, "We may never know the answer to this mystery. What we *can* know is a good life."

So the larger meaning is this: before we can find the answers to the great questions of existence, we must first remove human pain.

The mysteries of the universe will unfold forever. Our knowledge will expand forever, our mastery of technologies will expand forever, and our awareness of our own human nature will expand forever. We cannot neglect human well-being in favor of searching for answers in these areas, because there is no final conclusion to reach. Human life will expire before we are satisfied!

If we want humanity to survive to benefit from our discoveries, we must make the healing of existing suffering our first priority. Remember that it is within each short individual human lifetime that the opportunity to answer great questions lies. So we must heal human lives, heal the suffering of poverty and sickness and war. This is the ultimate value, repairing *now* any pain or problem that has already come into existence. If we go first to find the origin of the universe and let human life deteriorate, what good will the answers do us? An injured humanity cannot reveal great mysteries, or make use of the answers if they find them. The fascinating universe will not expire; it will unfold without our attention. But lives *do* expire, they *do* require our attention, and lives hold the answers we seek.

On a community level, when a person is suffering and we try to find out if it's their mother's fault or their father's, if it's the doing of society or if it's written in their genes, it won't help the person! These questions may intrigue us, but the solution to suffering is to take care of the person, to take care of their needs. We may never get to the bottom of those other concerns, and even if we find the answer, the suffering person still has gotten no benefit. For example, when a child commits an act of violence, and we begin to investigate the weapon, the school system, and the influence of television, we must remember that this does not actually heal anyone's pain! Wherever pain is present our job is to heal the pain, and then to look to the people involved to help answer our questions.

On a personal level, this is parallel to the person who says, "First I must sort out my career, then I'll be able to relax." Or, "If only I were married, then my life would make sense." We all do this at some time, thinking, "After I graduate, then things will be alright," or "If I can just figure out what went wrong, then I could move forward." It all amounts to, "As soon as I solve this problem, then I'll really be able to live." What will happen if you never get that particular desire? You will have held off your well-being for nothing!

Conquer your problems in the opposite order: First take care of your life. First remove your pains, learn how to live happily, and enjoy yourself as you are. Neglecting your well-being is counterproductive to finding answers, for it is your health and your happiness that lead to the discoveries you seek. So there is no need to solve the mysteries of your existence before caring for yourself and for others. You may never get to the bottom of how any situation in your life came to be. And whether you do or you don't, those answers matter very little next to healing your injuries and living well.

Buddha teaches us that we have priorities in problem solving: healing ourselves and those around us comes first; advancement of our understanding comes second. To the question "How did the universe come into being?" Buddha's amazing answer is, "Our lives are the important concern."

Socrates' Answer to the Mystery of Death

Around the year 400 BC, in Athens, Greece, the teacher Socrates was sentenced to death by poisoning. He was convicted of refusing to worship the Gods recognized by the city, and of teaching unpopular ideas. Socrates' many supporters begged him to escape from prison, but he refused.

On the day of his execution, his friends and students gathered around him in his prison cell. His best friend Crito sat beside him, his heart too heavy to speak. Though Socrates smiled easily at him, Crito gazed back with a horribly pained face. Socrates laughed.

"I cannot make Crito believe that I am the same Socrates as before. He's looking at me as I live, and seeing the dead body he shall soon see. Please assure him when I have gone that I depart completely from this world, and then he will suffer less at my death. Don't let him say at the funeral, 'here we lay Socrates,' for that is not true; you bury my body only."

Socrates went into another chamber to have a bath. When he came back the sun had nearly set, and everyone sat without saying much. Then the jailer came in, looking terribly guilty.

He said, "Socrates, you are the noblest, gentlest and best of anyone who ever came into this jail. So I'm sure you won't yell at me when I ask you to take the poison. I am only acting in obedience to the orders—it isn't what I want done." Then he burst into tears and left.

Socrates called after him, "Thank you, I will do as you say." Then he said to his friends, "Since I've been here that man has treated me as well as he could, and now see how generously he suffers on my account." Then to Crito, "We must do as he says. Have him bring the cup if it's prepared, and if not, ask him to prepare it."

Crito said, "But you do not have to take it yet! Others have waited until late at night, long after the jailer bids them take it."

Socrates said, "Maybe other people had something to gain by putting off the hour of their death, but I do not need to spare a life which is already forfeit. Do as I say."

So Crito went out and returned with the jailer, carrying the cup.

Socrates said to him, "My friend, you are experienced in these matters, tell me how best to proceed."

The jailer said, "You can walk around until your legs get heavy. Then lie down and the poison will take care of the rest."

Then Socrates, in the easiest manner, showing no sign of fear or hesitation, took the cup. And without the least change of color or expression, he drank the poison. Then his friends could not contain their sorrow. Seeing their beloved teacher finish the cup, they covered their faces and wept. They cried not mostly for Socrates, but for themselves, for having to part with a great friend. The only calm person in the room was Socrates.

He said, "Why are you all crying? I've heard that men are supposed to die in a peaceful environment. I sent away my wife and children so that there wouldn't be crying."

When they saw that the one who was dying was not upset, they were ashamed, and they stopped crying. Socrates walked around the room until his legs began to feel heavy, and then he lay down on the bed as the jailer had instructed him.

He felt his legs with his hands and observed aloud, "My feet are cold, and the coldness rising. When the poison reaches the level of the heart, it will be over."

Socrates covered himself with the sheet, and a moment later uncovered his face to ask Crito to pay a debt, a tithe to God he just then remembered he owed. Crito pledged to pay it, and asked him if there was anything else. By that time Socrates was gone.

Socrates' students did mourn their loss. But every time they wished their teacher had not died that day, they remembered certain words he spoke at his trial. And as each of them came to their own deaths, they remembered those same words. After he was sentenced and all was said, Socrates stood alone and faced the court. The jury that ordered his execution listened with interest; everyone in the room looked to him like attentive pupils in school.

He said, "Now there has come to me what is generally believed to be the last and worst evil. But let us reflect in another way, and we shall see there is great reason to believe that death could be good. For one of two things: either death is a sleep without dreams, or it is a migration to another realm where the dead are. If it is like a sleep, then death is a great gain, for then eternity will pass as only a single night. And if the soul joins with others who have gone before—then let me die again and again! What would anyone not give to converse with the greats of the past? Above all, I will be able to continue my search into knowledge; as in this world, in that. Now we go our separate ways—I to die, and you to live. Which is better only God knows."

This is one of the most famous stories of death in all of human history. Socrates has the most unusual perspective: he reasoned that death is either a sleep without dreams, or a reunion in another realm. Neither is to be feared, is it? Furthermore, he said that because we cannot know if death is better or worse than life, it can only be seen as a parting of ways. No religion or prophet in the world has given a more satisfying answer to the mystery of death!

In addition to his brilliant explanation, we can learn a lot from the final hours of Socrates' life. First he warned Crito against anticipating his absence, treating his friend like a corpse while he was still alive! This is very common, mourning the loss of a loved one while they are still with us. Socrates shows how illogical this is, for we rob ourselves of precious time in their presence—the very time we yearn for when they are gone. Socrates says, 'Enjoy me living as I live.' Then he says, 'and when I have gone, know that I depart completely.' This is a very comforting piece of advice. It means that after someone has died, there is no need to worry about them as if they still have the cares of a living person. We do no need to feel badly for our loved one as we look upon their body, for they are no longer living there!

Imagine the person you love saying, 'Enjoy me living as I live, and when I have gone, know that I depart completely.' Then you will not spend one moment of life in needless sorrow. See how Socrates comforted his friends; everyone around him was dreary even though he was not! The dying person is the one preparing to enter the unknown. If we love them, we can let them see the joyful faces of their friends. We can help them to feel happiness and satisfaction. Wouldn't you want to see strong, loving faces? Then each of us could die at peace like Socrates, with our friends focused on our well-being, giving support in same the way we want our friends to support us at birth, graduation, marriage, and other important rites.

Socrates was too intelligent to fear death. Because he was not afraid, he was able to enjoy the company of his friends and students. He was able to live fully to the last moment, open to life and interested in learning more. Look at the way he asked the jailer how to take the poison! He did not actually need instructions for this, but he asked the jailer anyway, treating him as an expert, in the hopes of learning something new. Socrates even wanted to track the progress of the poison inside his body as it killed him! No one would ask to die like this, but for Socrates it was easy.

His confidence in the jail cell shows that he truly believed what he said in the courtroom. He knew that life, which is filled with reason and good, could not possibly go to something inexplicably horrible. There is no *reason* to think it would, so Socrates didn't! He viewed his death as merely the next experience in his life, and even hoped to continue expanding his knowledge in another realm.

Socrates could have escaped from jail, lived more years, and died naturally. Certainly most of us would have chosen to do just that. Why did he choose to stay and accept such a fate? Incredibly, the man sentenced for teaching unusual ideas took his sentence as a great opportunity— the opportunity to teach one more idea that everyone should hear. It is this: we have no reason to believe death should be feared. Not only that, we have reason to believe it is good. Our powers of reason tell us to enjoy living while we live, and part ways when we must. Socrates offers us this perspective, both peaceful and profound, an invaluable gift for all who read his story.

Tolstoy Says: Celebrate Life!

The ambitious peasant Pakhom, after gaining ever greater plots of land, heard of the most incredible deal in a far-off country. He traveled to the land of the Bashkirs and negotiated with the village elder, who seemed to be a fool. The elder told Pakhom he could have all the land he wanted for a thousand rubles a day.

"A day?" said Pakhom, "What kind of rate is that? How many acres would that be?"

The elder said, "We don't reckon your way. We sell by the day. However much land you can walk around in one day will be yours, for the price of one thousand rubles."

Pakhom could hardly believe his ears.

"But I can walk around a lot of land in a day."

The elder burst out laughing.

"And all of it will be yours! There is only one condition: if you don't return to the starting point by sundown, your money will be forfeit."

Pakhom arranged to meet the villagers the next morning at daybreak to ride out to the appointed spot. Ecstatic, he spent a sleepless night. He knew he needed to rest but he could not stop thinking about the land. Rising before dawn, he went with the Bashkirs to the top of a hill.

The elder stretched out his arm in front of him.

"All of this land is ours, as far as the eye can see. And you may have any part of it that you like."

Pakhom's eyes glistened. The land was perfect in all four directions, the soil black and fertile. The elder took off his cap and placed it on the ground.

"This is the starting point," he said. "Return here by sunset."

Pakhom placed his thousand rubles on top of the cap and began to walk. He dug holes along the way to mark his land. All morning the going was easy, and he thought, "I'll go another three miles and then turn left. The land is so beautiful here, it would be a pity to miss any part."

The day grew warmer and Pakhom took off his jacket, then his boots. He stopped to drink water and eat a little bread. Walking again, Pakhom wondered if he had rested too long. The sun was now high, but he did not want to turn just yet. Pakhom picked up his pace, going out of his way to add more land. At noon he looked back to the hill where he had begun. It was difficult to see the people on top. He worried he had gone too far, and decided he must begin to plot shorter sides.

Pakhom turned and began to mark the second side. As the afternoon wore on, the heat became exhausting. By now his bare feet were cut and bruised, and his legs weakened. He wanted to rest again, but it was out of the question. He went on, telling himself, "An hour to suffer, a lifetime to live."

Pakhom struggled, walking faster, then running. He went along the third side, going out of the way for pieces of land he simply could not pass by, and cutting back in where he could. He worried that he had been too greedy, and his fear made him breathless. Now the sun was nearly halfway to the horizon, and looking back to the hill, Pakhom saw he was at least ten miles from the goal. Quickly he dug his last hole, and turned straight to the hill.

"Oh dear," he thought, "If only I had not blundered trying for too much! What if I am too late?

It was very hard going, but Pakhom went more and more quickly until he was running full speed. He threw away his coat, his boots, his flask, and his cap, keeping only the spade, which he used for support. On he ran, his shirt soaked and his throat parched. His lungs were working like a blacksmith's bellows, and his heart beat like a hammer. Pakhom was terrified.

He thought, "All this strain will be the death of me." Although Pakhom feared death, he couldn't stop. "They would call me an idiot," he thought.

When he was close enough to hear the Bashkirs cheering, he summoned his last ounce of strength and kept running. As finally he reached the hill, everything suddenly became dark—the sun had set.

Pakhom groaned miserably, "My labor has been in vain!"

He wanted to stop, but then he heard the Bashkirs still cheering him on. He realized that from where he was at the bottom of the hill, the sun had set—but it had not set for those on top. Pakhom took a deep breath and rushed up the hill, bending his body forward so his feet would have no choice but to catch him. Reaching the top, he saw the elder sitting by the hat, laughing his head off. Pakhom's legs gave way beneath him and he fell forward and reached the cap with his hands.

"Oh, that's a fine fellow!" exclaimed the elder. "That's a lot of land you've earned yourself!"

Pakhom's worker ran up and tried to lift his master, but Pakhom was dead. The worker picked up Pakhom's spade, dug a grave long enough for Pakhom to lie in, and buried him in it. Six feet from his head to his heels was all he needed.

Tolstoy's story is one of the finest ever written, showing us how to live life on this planet. One truth it contains is that life does not go on endlessly. To a young person life may seem like a gift of limitless land, but as we go on we remember that eventually we must return to our origin. Another truth is that we do not get to keep what we acquire in this life. This means that we do not need to acquire any amount of land so much as we need to enjoy the experience of walking around on it. If you do not celebrate living, but go running breathlessly after this and that, by the time you realize that you are going to die, there will be no time left to celebrate your life.

Pakhom could have kept to a pace he enjoyed. He could have cut himself enough land to live and work on, had a lovely day claiming it, and lived to enjoy another day. There is nothing wrong with acquiring property, or money, or success in business. There is also nothing wrong with working hard and exercising our abilities. However, it is very important to enjoy yourself while you are running after your goals. It is very important not to work so hard that you cannot fully enjoy each day.

There are many forces, internal and external, which will try to convince you that happiness will come to you once you acquire or accomplish what you desire. Do not believe it! No matter how far you go there will always be another goal you could achieve, something more you could do or acquire. We cannot put off enjoying ourselves until our work is finished, because there is no end to work. But there is an end to life, so *do not put off enjoying your life for even one moment*. Let your enjoyment guide you in your choices, and you will make choices that help you live to enjoy the next day.

Life is an experience to celebrate, not a store of items to possess. Tolstoy's story reminds us to stay in a spirit of celebration while we are toiling for wealth, property, status, etc., remembering that one day we must leave this planet, and leave all we've acquired here. This way, when death comes, you will know you spent your time wisely. Tolstoy titled this story "How Much Land Does a Man Need?" What he tells us is that we need very little land. What we need in large quantity is *life*—and life means celebrating the experience of being alive.

Christic the Judge

Early one morning Jesus went to the temple in Jerusalem. He sat on the steps and began to teach, and many people came to listen. When the leaders and officials of the temple saw what a crowd gathered to hear him speak, they decided to test Jesus' knowledge. They brought a woman accused of adultery to the place where Jesus sat.

They made her stand in front of the crowd, and one of the leaders said, "Teacher, this woman was caught in the very act of committing adultery. Now in the law, Moses commanded us to stone such women. What do you say?"

Jesus did not answer right away. He bent down and drew with his finger on the ground.

When the officials kept questioning him, he stood up and said to them, "Let anyone among you who is without sin be the first to throw a stone at her." Then he knelt down again and wrote on the ground.

When the officials thought about what Jesus said, they began to wander off, one by one, beginning with the elders.

Jesus was left alone with the woman still standing before him.

He stood up and asked her, "Woman, where are they? Has no one condemned you?"

She said, "No one, sir."

Jesus said, "Neither do I condemn you. Go your way, and from now on do not sin again."

————————

This is a very beautiful story about compassion. The established teachers came to test the judgment of a new teacher, and Jesus responded by showing a very high law indeed. The sin of adultery can represent any sin—any type of regrettable experience. And throwing a stone means condemning someone—judging someone in a way that brings doom to their life. Jesus told the people, 'Anyone free from negative experiences of their own can condemn this woman for her experience.' In other words, only someone who has never made a mistake is incapable of understanding what it is to make a mistake.

Then the teachers turned and walked away instead of picking up a stone. They thought of the mistakes in their own lives, perhaps the very same mistake made by the woman, and they considered if they should have been condemned for what they did. Then not one of them found within themselves the right to punish her, even though the law recommended it. No one could say a word, because of course every person has had some type of painful experience that they would like to leave behind.

The higher law of compassion tells us to consider if our own history of errors is truly beyond repair before judging someone else's as unforgivable. Everyone has made errors and everyone has regrets, and there is no one who cannot consider this when we encounter someone's error and must decide how to treat them. There is a beautiful detail included in this scripture—that the officials wandered off "beginning with the elders." People with many years' experience can easily see that no one would live long if mistakes were not allowed.

The way Christ judged was not to judge at all. Instead, the temple officials considered, understood, and learned to show mercy, because we all make mistakes.

Christis Interprets the Sabbath

Jesus traveled from town to town throughout Israel, teaching those who gathered to hear him. "One sabbath he was going through the cornfields; and as they made their way his disciples began to pluck heads of grain.

The Pharisees said to him, 'Look, why are they doing what is not lawful on the sabbath?'

And he said to them, 'Have you never read what David did when he and his companions were hungry and in need of food? He entered the house of God, when Abiathar was high priest, and ate the bread of the Presence, which it is not lawful for any but the priests to eat, and he gave some to his companions.' Then he said to them, 'The sabbath was made for humankind, and not humankind for the sabbath; so the Son of Man is lord even of the sabbath.' (Mark 2:23-28)"

The same question came to the teacher on another occasion: "Now he was teaching in one of the synagogues on the sabbath. And just then there appeared a woman with a spirit that had crippled her for eighteen years. She was bent over and was quite unable to stand up straight.

When Jesus saw her, he called her over and said, 'Woman, you are set free from your ailment.' When he laid his hands on her, immediately she stood up straight and began praising God.

But the leader of the synagogue, indignant because Jesus had cured on the sabbath, kept saying to the crowd, 'There are six days on which work ought to be done; come on those days and be cured, and not on the sabbath day.'

But the Lord answered him and said, 'You hypocrites! Does not each of you on the sabbath untie his ox or his donkey from the manger, and lead it away to give it water? And ought not this woman, a daughter of Abraham whom Satan bound for eighteen long years, be set free from this bondage on the sabbath day?' When he said this, all his opponents were put to shame; and the entire crowd was rejoicing at all the wonderful things that he was doing. (Luke 13:10-17)"

Now many people were interested in Jesus' new concept of the Sabbath. "Again he entered the synagogue, and a man was there who had a withered hand. They watched him to see whether he would cure him on the sabbath, so that they might accuse him.

And he said to the man who had the withered hand, 'Come forward.' Then he said to them, 'Is it lawful to do good or to do harm on the sabbath, to save life or to kill?' But they were silent. He looked around at them with anger; he was grieved at their hardness of heart and said to the man, 'Stretch out your hand.' He stretched it out, and his hand was restored. (Mark 3:1-5)"

The message in these passages is that we must design our laws to benefit human well-being. It is a timely message for people living in every part of the world, because laws and customs are a necessary part of every society. Jesus' people had forgotten that laws exist solely through our creating them, and Jesus reminded them to create their laws to serve their lives. "The sabbath is made for humankind" means that we are here to serve our fellow human beings, not to invent restrictions that prevent us from serving them, because "for humankind" means for the benefit of humankind.

There are three separate situations here showing health and well-being valued above a law which stands in the way of it. In the first story, Jesus tells the Pharisees of a time in their history when the human necessity for food took priority over a ritual use of food. In the second story, Jesus points out that we cannot logically withhold from a human the care we would give to an animal. And in the third, Jesus says that laws are meant to support our lives, not take away from them.

Humankind is responsible for the creation of our customs—what a powerful teaching! We have the power to ensure that laws are useful, the power to design our customs to enhance our lives. What good is a rule if we must give up health and wholeness in order to obey it? Why should a living being serve a ritual? This is what is meant by "so the Son of Man is lord even of the sabbath." Laws do not exist outside our will, rather we are their creators. So when a law becomes bondage or burden, we can change it! We can put rules in their proper place of serving us. Laws should be valued by their ability to support life. Our laws are our inventions, and they should be our assistance—they should assist us in the service of humankind.

I have long wondered how Christ was able to bring such a wonderful insight into the world. Let me share one more story, telling how Christ's interpretation of the sabbath came to be, and honoring the person who allowed his wisdom to live and grow:

Mother Mary's Gift of Light

When Jesus was a little boy, he saw his mother Mary giving food to the beggars and travelers who came passing through Nazareth. She gave them water, and the bread left over from her table. Jesus saw Mary do this many times—so many times that he learned to fetch the bread as soon as he saw a stranger in town.

One Sabbath evening, after the lamps were lit and the blessings said, Jesus asked his mother, "Why do you give bread to the beggars, even though we ourselves are poor?" Mary was surprised to hear her child say they were poor, and she sought to reassure him.

"Don't worry, Son, I will take care of you. You will always get enough to eat."

Then Jesus asked her, "If some beggars come tonight or tomorrow, will you stay inside, or will you go out?"

Mary said, "You know the law. We must stay inside to keep the Sabbath holy."

Jesus was quiet, and then he said, "What is holy when someone is hungry? Our blessings are made to be used, aren't they? Any day we use them could be called the Sabbath."

Mary was touched by Jesus' warmth of heart. She took him on her lap and held him, and tried to help him understand.

"You know that isn't the way it works," Mary said. "You know what is written: the Sabbath is from sundown to sundown."

Jesus said, "But Mom, I do not see how a law that keeps us from God's work can be God's law."

Mary was astounded. She thought over what he said, and she heard the truth in it.

"No, my child," said Mary, "I do not see that either."

After she put Jesus to bed, Mary went outside and sang a song to the night sky. She praised God for giving her life, and for giving her Jesus. From then on, Mary's family shared their food with hungry people on whichever day of the week they came.

Laila and Majnu, The Search for God Through Love

Twelve hundred years ago in ancient Persia, a poor man named Majnu fell in love with a beautiful woman named Laila. Not only was Majnu poor, he was also ugly, short in stature, and not very strong. He lived in the worst area of town, and he owned no property. He had no prospects for a career, and he was too young for anyone to respect him. Laila was the opposite. She was not merely pretty, she was gorgeous—she was like the winner of the Miss Universe pageant. Not only beautiful, she was also rich and famous, and she would be attended to and admired her entire life, because she was the daughter of the King of Persia. But truly, all of that was hardly worth mentioning in comparison to this: Laila and Majnu were born to love each other.

They met on the day Majnu came to the palace to beg for food. Laila's cart came to pause by the beggars on the ground and Laila looked down and saw Majnu. Immediately she knew that they must be together. You see, these two people were lovers in a past life, and in that past life they had a very deep relationship. The moment she met his gaze, Laila reconnected with the moment she parted from Majnu in the past. Majnu had the same powerful feeling, but his mind did not let him believe that a princess could love him. They looked into each other's eyes and saw only love. Then the cart moved on and the crowds came between them.

Laila thought of nothing but Majnu. She told her friends she had seen the man of her dreams, her Prince Charming, and they urged her to go look for him. Laila searched all throughout the city, and eventually she found Majnu living with one hundred other poor people in a slum across the river. Majnu turned and their eyes met again, and instantly they both felt the same joyful recognition. Laila told Majnu what she was feeling, and Majnu, whose heart was very loving, knelt down and returned the same promises to her.

Then Laila left the palace each morning singing happily to herself. She walked to the river and paid a coin to the boatman to row her across, and she and Majnu spent the day together. They left the city and walked in the shade of the trees, talking and learning from each other. First they discussed every topic in the world of interest to either one of them. Then they spoke from the heart about the things they cherished most dearly in life. At times what Laila had to say was so important that she would stop walking, take Majnu's hands and look into his eyes, in order to say it properly.

Laila visited Majnu every day, until her parents found out that their daughter, who was an heiress and celebrity, had fallen in love with a penniless and anonymous man. Then there was a big argument in her family, with everyone yelling and wailing, and it ended with Laila's parents forbidding her to see Majnu.

Laila did not even consider obeying her parents—instead she simply changed her schedule. Now she tiptoed out of the palace at night. She climbed over the back wall where the garbage was put out. She walked to the river, and with the boatman off duty, she took his boat and rowed herself across. She took care to be as silent as the stars in the sky, and no one noticed her.

Each evening Majnu went fishing in that same river. He built a fire and prepared a barbecue for Laila, and by the time she arrived he had a delicious meal ready for her. Then together they ate and laughed and celebrated. They continued their walks hand in hand, circling the campground in the darkness. At around three in the morning Laila left Majnu's tent, rowed back across the river, climbed over the wall, and returned to the palace before dawn.

But Laila's parents and friends were not stupid. They saw how she was sleepwalking through the days, and confronted her with her disobedience. They were beyond anger now; they absolutely could not fathom Laila's behavior.

They said, "How can you possibly care for this person? We've seen him, he's nothing special. What can you be thinking?"

Laila said, "Borrow my eyes. Only through my eyes can you see what I see, and then you will understand my love for dear Majnu."

That was her answer, and after that Laila's family could not stand in her way.

Laila and Majnu continued to meet, and their relationship continued to expand in all directions. Their love grew, as the poet Barrett Browning wrote, "to the depth and breadth and height my soul can reach." Laila jumped when she caught her reflection in the mirror. Somehow she expected to see Majnu's face there instead, and her own features startled her. Something similar happened to Majnu. The more perfectly he learned every detail of Laila's face, the less he could think what she looked like. When he looked upon her now, some other, brighter beauty shone out, and obscured whatever face it was he used to see. For both the lovers, setting eyes on each other ignited them within, and there was less and less to say. They met every night without fail, and each time Majnu greeted Laila with the best meal he could provide.

Then one day there was a violent thunderstorm, and the rivers flooded and scattered all the fish. Although he tried for hours, Majnu could not catch a single fish, or even a crab. The hour came for Laila to arrive, and Majnu could not greet her with nothing—by now Majnu was incapable of disappointing Laila. So he took his knife and cut a piece of flesh from his left thigh and cooked it for her. Can you imagine!? Laila came as usual, and she ate what Majnu offered her. There was no way for her to know; his leg was tied up with a cloth, and he was already seated when she arrived.

All she said was, "Today it doesn't taste like regular fish."

And all he said was, "Well, the river was flooded, so I found something else to serve you."

Just think—Laila would not have wanted food if there was none to be had; she did not visit Majnu in order to eat dinner. Majnu was the one close to starvation, and there he sat, satisfied to watch Laila eat. Just think—what kind of love that is!

So their life together continued, and Majnu rose to ever higher states of love. If he had had friends they would have passed him unknowing on the street; that is how completely he had changed.

One evening Laila made her walk down to the riverbank and found the boat missing. So she took off her clothes and tied them to a stick, and she held the stick aloft and entered the river. She swam across on her back, looking up at the sky and picturing the face of her love, relishing the anticipation of seeing him. On the other side of the river she put on her dress and made her way to Majnu's tent.

Something was different when Laila arrived. There was his tent and there was the fire. There was the fish hissing on the spit. And there was Majnu, sitting waiting for her as usual. But his eyes were closed.

He was chanting softly over and over, "Laila, Laila, Laila, Laila..."

Laila said, "It's me, I'm right here!" but Majnu did not open his eyes. He continued saying her name, and she said,

"You call my name and here I stand before you. Why don't you open your eyes?"

Then Majnu opened his eyes and looked at her. Slowly he closed his eyes then and opened them again, and then once more. Finally he dared to speak.

He said, "Today Majnu has become Laila. Today I could not wait for you, my dear. I wanted you so, and when I closed my eyes, there you were! You have been here for hours already. And now I see you within and without, eyes open and closed. How can this be? My love, I must have become *you. I don't think I need you anymore!"*

Laila sat close to Majnu. She took his hands in hers, looked in his eyes and said, "Majnu, what you speak of, this is what I have carried in my soul forever."

Like two rivers running toward the sea, Laila and Majnu had merged and become one. Then together they joined with a love neither imagined existed. Together they entered an immense ocean of love. Love like a tremendous tide pulled them into its depths, and then washed them out to its farthest limits, only it was limitless. Grown infinite as the universe, Laila and Majnu gazed into their eyes without saying a word, both of them unspeakably amazed, and shared in the silence between them the same vast, eternal love.

This is a love story with a deep meaning concerning the human search for God. Laila represents God, and Majnu represents a seeker of God. Whatever type of God we worship individually, our God is the highest possible experience, the highest expression of the spirit. Majnu was searching and striving for this satisfaction, and then he discovered God within himself.

In the beginning it was Laila that connected Majnu to the experience of highest love. Then Majnu found within himself the power to grant his connection with God. Majnu shows that once you discover connection to the source of the highest experience within yourself, then even if God knocks on your door, you will say, "Thank you for visiting me, God, but I don't need you to visit, because now I experience you all the time!"

We cease to seek when we become that which we seek. Majnu says, "What I was seeking, I have become that now." He lived for Laila to such a high level that one day he understood that loving her was the same as being her. How can you come closer to God than experiencing and expressing God? Even God arriving at your house for dinner is not so close! Once you express God, there is no more to seek. Like Majnu, we can express our divine love to such a high degree that finally after one day we say, "Now I don't search for God, because I experience God within me, and I cannot get any closer."

References

Attachment Invites Suffering
This is an ancient story from the oral tradition of India.

Acceptance of Negative Gifts Invites Pain
This story is found in the *Dhammapada*, quoted verses 3-4, 223. Available at http://www.gutenberg.org.

The Dancer Transforms The Demon
This story is found in an ancient Hindu text called *Shiva Purana*, meaning 'the history of Shiva,' originally written in Sanskrit. One publisher is Bangabasi Press, Calcutta, 1907. Also performed as a play or dance called "Mohini Bhasmasur," meaning 'the beautiful woman who destroyed the ash-demon.'

Shakespeare's verse from *The Merchant of Venice* (v, i, 83-85), available at http://www.gutenberg.org.

How Did the Universe Come into Being? Buddhist Answer

"The Parable of the Arrow" is from the *Dhammapada*, which means 'verses of truth' or 'paths of truth,' attributed to Buddha himself. Translation by F. Max Muller available at http://www.gutenberg.org.

Socrates' Answer to the Mystery of Death

Socrates' story is in a work called *Phaedo*, by Plato. This telling based on the translation by Benjamin Jowett, released 1999, available at http://www.gutenberg.org.

Tolstoy Says: Celebrate Life!

How Much Land Does a Man Need? by Leo Tolstoy, 1886. This telling based on the translation by Aylmer Maude, Louise Shanks Maude in *What Men Live By and Other Tales*, released 2004, available at http://www.gutenberg. org.

Christ the Judge

"The Woman Caught in Adultery," paraphrased from John 7:53-8:11, *New Testament Bible*, available at http:// bible.oremus.org, New Revised Standard Version.

Christ Interprets the Sabbath

The quoted passages are from the *New Testament Bible*, available at http://bible.oremus.org, New Revised Standard Version.

Laila and Majnu, The Search for God Through Love

The tale of Laila and Majnu comes from ancient Arabian and Persian folklore. Versions as a story or a play may be titled "Majnun Layla," meaning 'driven mad by Laila.'

Quote from Elizabeth Barrett Browning's "Sonnet XLII" from *Sonnets from the Portuguese* available at http://www. gutenberg.org.

About the Authors

Amarjit Singh Modi is a world-renowned palmist, psychic, meditation teacher and healer. Born and raised in Kashmir, India, he realized at an early age that his calling was to teach and inspire others. With forty years experience in the spiritual arts, Singh Modi has acquired a vast knowledge of the holy scriptures and writings of all the world's religions. He has read more than fifty thousand palms in one hundred eighty-nine countries. His journey to spiritual enlightenment has taken him all over the globe, and his love of people has made him several hundred friends on each continent. He shares with each one the wisdom he has gained from his life and study, and in doing so empowers people to live life as the adventure it is. One of Mr. Modi's primary tasks in this life is to prepare the planet for the coming messiah. He believes that she will be a woman; a musician from the Middle East, coming to restore peace and harmony to the planet by balancing the male and female energies. He lives in New York City since 1971.

Elizabeth Temple also lives in New York City. From *The Heart to The Mind* is her second book with Mr. Modi.